Folk Tales of Old Japan

Sumie Illustration by Mitsuo Shirane

The **Japan Times**, Ltd.

ISBN4-7890-0033-8

Copyright © 1975   All rights reserved
First edition, June 1975
Fifth printing, September 1986

Compiled by The Publications Dept., The Japan Times, Ltd.
Sumie illustration by Mitsuo Shirane

Published by The Japan Times, Ltd.
5-4, Shibaura 4-chome, Minato-ku, Tokyo 108, Japan

Printed in Japan

Preface

This is a collection of 16 Japanese folk tales which have been told and retold by our ancestors through the centuries and which still remain popular among Japanese children today.

Every nation has its own folk tales. Such stories leave indelible impressions in the minds of the people and exert significant effects on character formation of respective nations.

The folk tales presented in this volume represent the cream of Japanese literary creations of this genre and form a common cultural property of the Japanese people.

We hope that these stories will provide foreign readers with a key to understanding Japanese cultural traditions, customs and manners. Each story is accompanied by two ''sumie'' illustrations designed to help the reader better appreciate the flavor of the tale.

Except ''Kachi-kachi Yama'' and ''Hana-saka Jijii,'' the stories included in this volume have been reproduced from a series titled ''Folk Tales of Old Japan'' which was published in the Information Bulletin (June, 1971-March, 1972), a fortnightly report issued by the Public Information Bureau, Ministry of Foreign Affairs, Japan.

CONTENTS

The Peach Boy

(Momotaro)

LONG, long ago, there lived an old man and an old woman. Every day, the old man went to the mountains to gather brushwood, while the old woman went to a nearby stream to wash clothes.

One day, while the old woman was doing the day's washing, a huge peach came floating down the stream. She picked up the peach, which was so big she had to carry it with outstretched arms around it, and in this way brought it home. As soon as the old man returned from the mountains, the old woman took out a kitchen knife to prepare the peach for eating. All of a sudden, however, the peach split in two of itself and with a loud cry out came a cute baby boy. The old man and woman were so surprised they fell back in awe and wonder.

Yet the old couple was extremely delighted, as they

7

had no child. They named the boy Momotaro ("Momo" means peach, and "Taro" is one of the commonest names for Japanese boys) because the baby was born of a peach. And the old man and woman brought up the boy with tender care.

Momotaro grew with marvelous speed as each bowl of rice he ate rendered him that much bigger. And as everything he ate added to his growth, Momotaro soon became a big boy with power unequalled in the neighborhood.

One day, Momotaro knelt down politely in front of the old man and woman and bowed his head deeply. "I want to go to 'Onigashima' (the Ogres' Island) to conquer the demons who frighten the people so. Please let me go!" he said. The old man and woman were surprised and worried and at a loss how to answer. At the repeated urging of Momotaro, however, they finally gave their consent, made millet dumplings and put them into a bag as meals for the boy.

Momotaro left home in high spirits. At the end of the village, he chanced upon a dog. "I know you are Momotaro-san. Where are you off to ?" asked the animal. "I'm going to 'Onigashima' to subdue the demons," an-

swered the boy. "Then, what are you carrying there by your
side?" asked the dog. "The best millet dumplings in
Japan!" replied Momotaro.

The dog asked him for a dumpling, and Momotaro
agreed on condition the dog accompany him on the devil-
conquering expedition. The dog obliged, received a dumpling and went along with Momotaro. Soon the party came
across a pheasant, which also agreed to join the expedition
upon receiving a millet dumpling. Next the party met a

9

monkey, which similarly agreed to help Momotaro in exchange for a dumpling.

Now Momotaro crossed over to Onigashima with the dog, pheasant and monkey as retainers.

Upon reaching the island, Momotaro found a giant gate, firmly closed, standing in his way. But the pheasant took to the air, flew over the gate and opened it from inside. Momotaro and his party passed through the gate and found the demons in the midst of a revelry.

"Listen!" Momotaro shouted. "I am Momotaro and I've come to punish you demons, who have plagued my fellow countrymen!" With this as a signal, the dog, pheasant and monkey pounced upon the drunken demons. Momotaro and each of his animal retainers now had the strength of a thousand men because they had eaten the "best millet dumplings in Japan!"

The pheasant pecked the demons' faces, the monkey scratched them and the dog bit their legs. Flustered, the demons fled to and fro. Finally overpowered, all of them surrendered. The chief demon knelt down in front of Momotaro and said with tears streaming from his big eyes:

"I beseech you to spare my life! I'll never do any harm to human beings again! And I'll give you all the treasures we have gathered here!"

The chief ordered his retainers to take the treasures, which had all been stolen from human beings, out of the storehouses and had them hauled to Momotaro.

Thereupon, Momotaro had the treasures loaded onto a cart and triumphantly set out for home with the dog and the pheasant pulling the cart and the monkey pushing it from behind.

The Old Man Who Had His Wen Removed by Goblins

(Kobu-tori Jiisan)

ONCE upon a time, there lived an old man with a wen on his forehead. The wen was as large as a fist. One day, he went into the mountain to work, but was overtaken by a violent rainstorm. Unable to walk on, he had no alternative but to stay in the mountain overnight. But he could find no woodcutter's hut. The rainstorm gained in intensity after nightfall. Frightened, the old man was at a loss what to do.

Fortunately, he found a giant tree with a large hollow in the trunk. He promptly entered the cavity. Shivering with cold and hunger, he squatted down, unable to sleep. Soon, a strange sound began to be heard from the distance. The sound gradually approached. Dumbfounded, he was scared stiff, his teeth chattering with terror. Looking out, he found the sound to be "kagura" (dance music dedicated to the gods) performed by several

13

"tengu" (a red-faced goblin with a long nose), each standing two meters tall.

Coming beside the tree in which the old man had hidden himself, the goblins sat down in a circle, made a fire, warmed "sake" (rice wine) and began dancing to the tune of "kagura."

Holding his breath, the old man watched the dance with a mixture of curiosity and fear. Not only did the goblins excellently perform "kagura" music with drums and flutes, but they also danced superbly with an exquisite movement of the hands. As they drank their "sake," they got more and more jovial, and the "kagura" dance went on and on.

At first, the old man, astonished and scared, could not stop his quivering. But as he continued to be enveloped by the pleasant rhythm of the "kagura" music, he soon forgot the danger he was exposed to and felt like going out of the hollow and dancing together with the goblins. Several times, he managed to contain such a desire and kept on peeping out of the tree trunk. Finally, however, spellbound by the charm of the "kagura" dance, he left the hollow, joined a ring of dancing goblins and started to dance himself.

Astounded, the goblins wondered what had happened, but soon, the old man's skillful dancing captivated them. They praised his dance, saying they had never before seen such an exquisite dancer. They ordered the old man to come again the next night and dance. Thanking them for the praise, he promised to come back. But a distrustful goblin said: "Well, I don't think his promise is a sufficient guarantee. Let us take something in pledge." They studied the old man's face, wondering what could be

the best pledge. Soon, they shouted with one accord: "That's it!" and pointed their fingers at the wen on his forehead. Thereupon, one of them snatched the wen off his face. Strangely enough, the wen came off without any pain and left no trace.

Soon, cocks started to crow in the distance and the day broke. Thereupon, the goblins disappeared no one knows where. Greatly delighted, the old man scampered down the mountain. Upon returning home, he told the whole story to his wife.

Living next door was another old man who also had a wen the size of a fist on his forehead. But this man was a very jealous fellow. Upon hearing his neighbor had had his wen snatched off by goblins, he made up his mind to have his wen removed in the same way.

As night fell, he went to the mountain and waited in the hollow of the tree for the goblins to turn up. Exactly as his neighbor had said, the goblins appeared and started their "kagura" dance. Though scared, the old man joined the ring of dancing goblins.

As it turned out, however, he was a poor hand at dancing. Disappointed and infuriated, the goblins shouted: "What a poor dancer you are! How can you dance so

17

differently from last night? Return him the wen we took in pledge last night!" When they hurled the wen at the dancing old man, it promptly attached itself to the top of his own wen. And this jealous old man had to live with a double-decked wen thereafter.

The Crab's Revenge

(Sarukani Gassen)

ONCE upon a time, there was a crab carrying a rice ball, and a monkey with a persimmon seed in his hand who happened to pass by. Very hungry, the monkey wanted very much to get the rice ball. "Dear crab," he said to the crab, "how about exchanging your rice ball for my persimmon seed?" Naturally, the crab would not consent to such a lop-sided proposition.

But the cunning monkey insisted in a coaxing voice: "The rice ball, once eaten, will be gone! By contrast, if you put the persimmon seed in the ground, it will soon put forth a shoot, which will grow to be a tall tree and bear fruit in the future. Then you can eat as many persimmons as you like. So let's make a swap!" His glib tongue finally cajoled the crab into exchanging the rice ball for the persimmon seed. The monkey lost no time in

19

eating the rice ball, while the crab took the persimmon seed home and planted it in a corner of his garden.

Every day after that, the crab brought out a spade, went to the corner of the garden where the persimmon seed was buried and sprinkled water on it, saying: "Unless you put out a shoot, I'll dig you out with this spade!" Afraid of being dug out, the persimmon seed put forth a shoot very early. Then the crab went to it with scissors and said: "Unless you grow fast, I'll chop you off with these scissors!" And again fearful of being chopped off, the persimmon sapling grew fast to be a tall tree. Thereupon, the crab brought out an ax and said: "Unless you bear fruit, I'll fell you down with this ax!" Again flustered, the persimmon tree bore fruit on all branches. And the tree suddenly became loaded with fruit all over.

Soon autumn arrived. The persimmon fruit ripened, displaying an appetizing red color. The monkey came, climbed up the tree, sat in a crotch and snatched off and ate the sweet, delicious fruit. Noticing this, the crab came and said to the monkey: "I can't climb up the tree, so please pluck a ripe fruit and give it to me." "All right," replied the monkey. He snatched off a green immature fruit and threw it at the crab. Thereupon the crab took a

bite but it tasted too sour. "Give me a sweeter one," implored the crab. But the monkey plucked another green persimmon and hurled it at the shell of the crab. Wounded, the crab had to take to his bed.

The crab had cute little children. With their parent bedridden, they spent every day crying with sorrow. Deeply moved by compassion, a hornet promised the little crabs to help them avenge their parent. Promptly, the hornet, buzzing around, spread the news. Thereupon, a chestnut, a sewing needle and a stone mortar offered to help.

Then the little crabs and their friends went to the monkey's home to avenge the parent crab. Fortunately, the monkey was out. So they immediately assigned roles to each other. The chestnut hid himself in a floor-hearth, the little crabs in a water jar in the kitchen, the hornet in a bean paste pot, the needle in the monkey's bedclothes, and the stone mortar on the roof above the entrance, lying in wait for the monkey.

In the evening, the monkey came home. Grumbling, "How cold it is," he sat down by the floor-hearth to warm himself. Thereupon, the heated chestnut burst open with a crack and hit the monkey's bottom. Severely burned, the monkey hastily ran to the kitchen and lifted the lid off the water jar to sprinkle water on the burn. At that moment, the waiting little crabs nipped the monkey's hand with their pincers. Startled, the monkey then took the lid off the bean paste pot, remembering bean paste is good for curing a burn.

Promptly, the hornet buzzed out and stung him all over. Utterly at a loss for what to do, the monkey hurried

into the bedclothes. But the sewing needle pricked him here and there. "Ouch, ouch! I can find no place to hide myself in my own home." Crying, he ran to the entrance to get out of the house. Thereupon, the stone mortar, until then quietly watching the flustered monkey flee about confused, jumped onto the monkey with a thud and pinned him down. Groaning with extreme pain, the monkey finally said: "Pardon me, please! I'll never do a bad thing again!" Thus he apologized and vowed to be good over and over again.

24

A Fisherman and the Sea Princess

(Urashima Taro)

LONG, long ago, a young fisherman by the name of Urashima Taro was living a modest life with his old mother.

One autumn, chilly north winds kept on blowing every day, making the sea so choppy that the man could not go out fishing. He was totally at a loss as he could not find enough food for his mother.

One day, high north winds of the previous night came to a stop and the sea became calm again before dawn. Delighted, Urashima set out to sea well before daybreak.

Oddly enough, however, his fish hook did not catch even a single small fish as the sun rose in the east and reached the middle of the sky. Finally as the sun was about to set in the west, his hook caught what appeared to be a big fish. Elated, he pulled it up. But what came up from the sea was a giant turtle!

Urashima released the turtle into the sea, thinking nobody would buy such a big turtle.

After nightfall, he pulled his boat ashore and returned home along a dark road without a single fish.

The next day, north winds again made the sea rough, making it impossible to go fishing. Sadly watching the choppy waters, Urashima walked along the beach. All of a sudden, the giant turtle Urashima had freed the day before raised its head between the waves.

"Dear Mr. Urashima," said the turtle. "Thank you for saving me yesterday! As a token of thanks, I would like to take you to the Dragon Palace." (The Dragon Palace is the residence of the Sea God at the ocean's bottom. Made of gold and silver, it is surrounded by beautiful gardens, full of colorful flowers and fruits, chirpings of pretty birds and exquisite music with singing and dancing beauties, fine wine and foods galore. It was considered a utopia of pleasure and longevity by ancient people.)

"Please get on my back! I am happy to guide you," said the turtle.

Though fascinated by what the turtle said, Urashima hesitated, thinking of his old mother. But the turtle said

assuringly: "Don't worry! We'll be gone for only two or three days!" So Urashima sat astride the creature.

The turtle with Urashima on its back dived into the sea. For a while, it swam through a misty area, but soon reached a gate near the gorgeous Dragon Palace. Immediately, the Princess of the palace accompanied by ladies in waiting, all beautifully dressed, came out with a host of fishes to greet Urashima amid the exquisite sound of music.

The whole of the palace personnel heartily welcomed Urashima with sumptuous banquets, cordial services by pretty ladies in waiting, charming dances of fishes and various other entertainments. Spellbound by such a cordial reception, Urashima, who at first intended to stay at the palace only a few days, after all spent as long as three years there.

When Urashima finally told the Princess he must be leaving for home, she handed him a three-tiered "Tamatebako" (jeweled hand-box), saying: "Please open the box when you are at a loss." With the box under his arm, Urashima got on the back of the turtle again and departed for home.

28   Upon reaching his home village, he found the shape

of mountains and rivers there had changed, while some of the trees on the hill were gone and others were withering. Wondering how such a marked change could have happened in only three years, he walked on toward his home.

Soon he noticed an old man he did not know working on a farm. "I used to live around here before, but don't you know a man by the name of Urashima Taro?" said Urashima to the old man. "Well," replied the man, "I once

heard that during the days of my grandfather, a man named Urashima Taro went to the Dragon Palace. But I was told that he did not come back after that." Needless to say, Urashima's mother was already long dead.

When he reached the place where he had lived, his house was nowhere to be found, and only the garden remained, overgrown with weeds.

Urashima was at a loss what to do, now that the people and nature of his home village had completely changed. Recalling the jeweled hand-box received from the Princess, he opened it. He found a crane's feather in the upper box. Then when he lifted the lid of the second box, a waft of white smoke rose leisurely from it. When enveloped by the smoke, Urashima suddenly turned into a white-haired old man bent with age.

And in the third box, he found a mirror. Looking into the mirror, he was astonished to find he had changed into an old man. While he was wondering what had happened, the crane's feather in the first box was swept into the air by wind. As soon as the feather landed on Urashima's back, he suddenly turned into a crane.

As the Urashima-turned-crane started to fly high into the sky, the giant turtle appeared again on the sea and watched the crane fly away into the distance. The turtle, it is said, was actually an incarnation of the Princess of the Dragon Palace.

The Rabbit and
The Raccoon Dog
(Kachi-kachi Yama)

ONCE upon a time, an old man and his wife lived happily together in a countryside village.

One day, the old man went out to the fields to work as usual, but found all his crops damaged and destroyed. Convinced that it was a raccoon dog that had played havoc with his crops, he set a trap for the animal in the farm.

Early next morning, he went to the spot where the trap had been laid, and found, as he had expected, a big raccoon dog ensnared. He caught and tied the animal with rope, brought him home and hung him from the ceiling. He then returned to the fields after telling his wife that the animal's meat would be ideal for the day's supper.

While he was away on the farm, the old woman began to prepare supper. The wily raccoon dog, seeing her hard at work, said to her: "Dear lady, your work seems too heavy for you to do alone. I want to help you, so please untie me!" The good-natured old woman, never doubting the animal's offer of help, set him free. But the raccoon dog promptly grabbed a large pestle he found in the room and severely beat up the old woman. He then fled into a nearby mountain.

The old man, upon returning home from the fields, was surprised to see his wife moaning with pain from her

wounds. Weeping with grief, he cared for the old woman day after day.

Deeply moved upon hearing this news, a rabbit living in a nearby burrow said to the old man: "All right, I shall punish the raccoon dog for you!"

One day, the rabbit called the wily raccoon dog out and went into the mountains together with him to collect wood for fuel. After gathering much firewood, the two set out homeward, each with a large bundle of wood on his back. The rabbit let the raccoon dog lead the way. He then struck a flint with steel, setting fire to the bundle of wood on the raccoon dog's back. When the flint was struck, it sounded "kachi, kachi" (click-clack). Wondering where the sound came from, the raccoon dog asked the rabbit about it. "Well, this is Mt. Kachi-kachi. That's why such a sound is heard around here, I think," replied the rabbit. Soon, the fire engulfed the bundle of wood carried by the raccoon dog, inflicting a heavy burn on his back.

When the raccoon dog's burn was almost healed, the rabbit came again and suggested the two go boating out to sea. The rabbit offered the use of his boat made of clay.

The raccoon dog, though still smarting from the bitter experience of suffering a burn on Mt. Kachi-kachi, gladly

accepted the invitation to go boating, thinking there would be no such danger on the sea.

The two animals rowed out to sea, the rabbit in a wooden boat and the raccoon dog in the clay boat. Soon, the clay boat was softened by the water and holes appeared here and there on the bottom. Sea water welled up through the holes, and the raccoon dog's boat began to sink. The animal was thrown into the sea, and unable to swim, he called the rabbit to help him. Thereupon, the rabbit said to him: "I shall save you if you pledge never to harass the old man and woman again!" The raccoon dog made the pledge and was barely saved from drowning.

The Old Man Who Made Dead Trees Bloom

(Hana-saka Jijii)

LONG, long ago, there lived an old man and woman who were honest and kind-hearted. But next door to them lived a wicked and greedy old couple.

The good old man had made a pet of a dog. One day, the dog led him to a patch of garden at the back of his house and barked earnestly as if to say: "Dig here! Dig here!" Realizing what the dog meant, the old man immediately dug the ground with a spade. To his great surprise, he found a lot of "oban" and "koban" (large and small gold coins of feudal Japan) and precious stones.

The old man brought the discovered treasure into his home. As he and his wife were examining and counting the find, the greedy old man next door happened to drop in. Astonished at the mountain of gold coins and precious stones, he asked the good old man what had happened.

Told about his neighbor's good luck, he borrowed the dog and took it to a garden behind his own house.

The greedy old man dug the spot where the dog barked. But far from finding gold coins, he was shocked to see a host of loathsome creatures — snakes, lizards, frogs, centipedes, etc. — creep out from under the ground. Deeply disappointed and infuriated, he killed the dog, buried it in the garden and stuck in a willow tree twig to mark the spot.

As the dog did not return for hours, the good old man became worried. He went to the wicked neighbor and heard what he had done to the poor dog.

The next day, he went to the spot where the dog was interred, in order to console its spirit. But he was amazed to find the willow twig had grown overnight into a giant tree about two arm lengths around. The good old man felled the tree and made a mortar out of its trunk. When he and his wife put steamed rice in the mortar and pounded it to make "mochi" (rice cake), a large number of "oban" and "koban" gold coins came pouring out of the mortar to their great surprise.

It so happened that the greedy old neighbor was peeping in at the time. He asked to borrow the mortar and

took it back home. When he started to pound rice in the
mortar with his wife, one filthy thing after another came
out, such as discarded old roof tiles and broken utensils —
but never the gold coins he wished to get! Incensed, the
greedy man burned the mortar in his kitchen range.

When the good old man came to get back the mortar,
it had already been reduced to ashes.

Resigned to his loss, he accepted instead part of the
ashes. On his way home, a small amount of the ashes

39

spilled from the palm of his hand, falling onto withered grass. At that instant, the grass flowered into fresh green! Heartened, the good old man climbed up a tree in his garden as soon as he returned home and sprinkled the ashes all around. Instantly, all trees in the vicinity — even dead ones — put forth beautiful flowers as if the floral season of spring had come round ahead of time. Impressed with the good old man's magical performance, all people in the neighborhood applauded him and called him "Hana-saka-jijii" (Old Man Who Makes Trees Flower).

His jealousy aroused by this, the greedy old man took out the remaining ashes from the kitchen range and climbed a tree in his garden to emulate the feat of his neighbor. Many people in the neighborhood gathered around to wait for dead trees to flower. However, the ashes scattered by him, far from making dead trees blossom, were merely-blown about by a gust of wind, smarting the eyes of the watching crowd. The enraged spectators punished him roundly.

The Old Couple and The Sparrow

(Shita-kiri Suzume)

ONCE upon a time, there lived an old man and woman.

One day, the old man went to a mountain, hung his lunch box from a tree branch and set to work. Soon noontime came and the old man opened the lunch box only to find it empty. The rice was gone and instead, a sparrow, which had eaten the lunch, was dozing contentedly with a full stomach. How cute the bird looked! The old man, forgetting about his own empty stomach, wrapped up the lunch box, containing the sparrow, brought it home and reared the bird affectionately.

A few days later, the old man again went to the mountain, leaving his wife and the little sparrow at home. The old woman made starch for washing clothes, placed it on the veranda and started to do her laundry by a well.

The sparrow pecked at the starch in the dish and found it very tasty. Another peck and still another — the bird, unable to resist the taste, went on pecking at the starch. Soon the starch vanished and only the cleanly licked dish remained. "Oh my," repented the bird, but it was too late.

With her washing finished, the old woman returned to the veranda but found no trace of starch. Dismayed, she searched about for the starch, but nowhere was it discovered. Puzzled and dejected, she casually looked at the end of the veranda. There, the sparrow stood still with a drooping head as if to apologize. The old woman raised the bird in the palm of her hand and, looking closely at its face, found a trace of starch on its bill. She opened the bird's mouth and also noticed a remnant of starch on its tongue. When she realized the starch she had made so carefully had been eaten up by the bird which she had been caring for so tenderly, she was suddenly overwhelmed with anger and on the spur of the moment took up a pair of scissors nearby and snipped off the bird's tongue.

Shrieking with pain, the sparrow flew from the hand of the old woman, who stood stupefied by what she herself had done in a fit of anger, and disappeared no one knows

43

where.

Shortly thereafter, the old man came back home.

"Well, my dear, how's the little sparrow?" he said to his wife. When the old woman told him what had happened, he said: "What a pity! I'll go and look for the bird." The old man then trudged back to the mountain.

"Where's the sparrow's home? Where's the home of the poor little sparrow who had its tongue snipped off?" Repeating this like a song, he searched through the mountain. He met a man herding cattle and asked him about the sparrow's home. Then he also met a man herding horses and put the same question to him, but to no avail.

Finally, however, he learned that the sparrow's home was located in a bamboo grove. Greatly delighted, he went into the grove.

At the sparrow's home, he found the bird weaving on a loom. "I'm very sorry you had your tongue chopped off!" said the old man. "Welcome, old man!" said the sparrow, and all the members of the bird's family came out to greet him. They heartily entertained him with a sumptuous dinner and "sparrow dances," and showed him various novelties. At nightfall, the old man said: "I must be leaving now, as my wife must be worried." "It's quite a pity

that you must go," said the sparrows. "Then old man, please accept whichever of these two you like as our gift." They brought two boxes, one large and the other small. "I'm old, you know, so I'd like to accept the smaller one," he said and bade them farewell, carrying the box on his back.

Upon returning home, the old man said to his wife: "I met the sparrow and received a gift. As I was asked which of the large and small boxes I preferred, I took the small one." So saying, he opened the box. Well, what do you think was in it? To his surprise, the box was packed with gold coins, large and small, gold and silver bullion, and various other treasures.

The old woman's initial surprise turned into greed. "Well, if I had been there, I would have taken the larger box!" she said. The next day, she went to the mountain herself to visit the sparrow's home after asking the old man about its location.

"Where's the sparrow's home? Where's the sparrow's home?" Repeating this, she went to the bird's home in the bamboo grove.

"My dear sparrow, I have also come to see you!" she said. "Welcome, old lady!" said the sparrow. And the

sparrow's family again entertained her with a sumptuous dinner and "sparrow dances," and showed her various novelties as had been the case with the old man. When the parting time came, they again brought two boxes, large and small, and asked her to take whichever she pleased.

"Well," said the old woman, "I would accept the larger one." With the help of the sparrows, she put the large box on her back and trudged down the mountain

47

road. On her way home, she took down the box on the road, what with its heavy weight and a growing curiosity about its contents, and raised the lid. What on earth did she find? Out came a swarm of snakes, lizards and ghosts! Startled, she jumped with fright and, half paralyzed with terror, crawled back home.

A Midget Who Defeated Goblins

(Issun-boshi)

LONG, long ago, a man and wife lived happily somewhere in Japan, but they had no children. One day, they went to a shrine and prayed fervently: "Oh God, please bless us with a child even if it is as small as a finger tip!"

Shortly after, the wife gave birth to a fine baby boy, but the baby was smaller than the finger of an adult man. Even so, the couple brought him up dearly as he was the apple of their eye.

The boy became a very sagacious, good-natured child, but his stature did not increase one bit. The boy was liked by all people in the neighborhood, who called him "Issun-boshi." (Literally, "issun" means one "sun"—about 3.3 centimeters — and "boshi" or "hoshi" a priest; in ancient times, many boys had their heads shaven like a

49

priest, so they were called "hoshi" and this gradually became a popular boy's name.)

One day, Issun-boshi thought of going to Kyoto, the Imperial capital, and rising to a high position.

So he said to his parents: "Father and mother, I intend to go to the capital and see and learn various things so that I may become a great man. Therefore, would you please give me leave for some time?" Though somewhat concerned, the parents gave him their ready consent, because they trusted the boy's sagacity. They made a tiny sword out of a sewing needle, put it into a sheath made of straw and hung it at the boy's waist. They also gave him a bowl and a chopstick.

Issun-boshi set out immediately. There was a river leading down to the capital. Using the bowl as a ship and the chopstick as the oar, he navigated down the stream for many days, finally arriving at the capital.

He walked about the capital and came to a large, magnificent residence, where a Minister of great influence lived. At the entrance, Issun-boshi shouted: "Hello, there! Hello, there!" A servant promptly came out but saw nobody at the entrance. Puzzled, he was about to turn back when he again heard someone shout; "Hello, there!

Hello, there!" The voice came from the direction of a pair of high clogs at the entrance. When the servant moved the clogs, he found Issun-boshi standing there.

"My name is Issun-boshi, and I have come to the capital to study. Please let me join the Minister's retainers," said Issun-boshi. His interest aroused by this strange tiny dwarf, the servant picked up Issun-boshi with two fingers and took him to the Minister.

When placed on the palm of the Minister's hand, Issun-boshi sat down squarely and decorously and bowed deeply. This impressed the Minister and all his staff so much that the Minister decided to make the dwarf his retainer and let him live at his residence.

Though very tiny, Issun-boshi was very wise and did every job smartly. Above all, he was very cute. Therefore, he soon became highly popular with all people at the Minister's residence. Especially, he became such a favorite with the Minister's daughter that she always kept him at her side.

One day, the daughter went to Kiyomizu to worship at the temple of the Kannon (Goddess of Mercy), accompanied by Issun-boshi. On their way home, two goblins, lying in wait, suddenly jumped forth and tried to

Mitsuo
Ikirané

kidnap the daughter. Issun-boshi, until then riding in a
sleeve of her dress, promptly leaped to the ground.
Drawing his needle sword, he shouted: "Who do you
think I am? I am Issun-boshi guarding the Minister's
daughter!" However, one of the goblins swiftly swallowed
him down.

Issun-boshi was so small that he could move around
freely in the goblin's stomach. Wielding his needle sword
at random, he pricked the inside walls of the stomach here

53

and there. Pained and startled, the goblin disgorged Issun-boshi. Thereupon, the other goblin tried to catch and squash Issun-boshi. But the dwarf leaped up to the goblin's eyebrow and plunged his needle sword into the goblin's eyes. Blinded and pained, the goblin with giant tears dripping fled with his colleague.

When he was about to take the Minister's daughter home who was then crying by the roadside, Issun-boshi found a small mallet left behind by the goblins. This was the goblins' treasure called "Uchide-no-kozuchi" (Mallet of Luck) and one could make it produce whatever one pleased simply by swinging it. Highly flustered in their flight, the goblins had forgotten the magic treasure. Issun-boshi picked it up and showed it to the Minister's daughter.

"Dear Issun-boshi," she said. "This is 'Uchide-no-kozuchi' and you can get whatever you like — money, rice or anything — from it!" But Issun-boshi said: "I want neither money nor rice. I just want to get my height increased!" Swinging the mallet, the daughter said: "Increase Issun-boshi's height! Increase!" Thereupon, Issun-boshi grew taller and taller, finally becoming a handsome young samurai (warrior).

Later, Issun-boshi, now a fully grown samurai, married the Minister's daughter and lived happily with his parents.

The Grateful Raccoon Dog

(Bunbuku Chagama)

ONCE upon a time, there lived an old man and woman, who were very poor. The old man went to the mountains every day to gather firewood and sold it in town to eke out a scanty livelihood.

One day, on his way to the mountains, he saw three village boys torturing a raccoon dog they had captured. Moved to pity, he said to the boys: "You mustn't treat a living thing so hard. Won't you sell it to me?" When he handed them some money, the boys gladly turned the creature over to the old man and went away.

The old man undid a rope tied around the neck of the raccoon dog and said: "What a pity! Never come close to the village again in broad daylight so that you may not be caught and roughed up again! Now, hurry back to your burrow!" And he released the animal into a wood.

56

Days and months passed, and the old man gradually forgot about the raccoon dog. The end of the year drew near, and the old man went to the mountains to gather firewood as usual, pondering how to make money to prepare for the New Year. Suddenly, a raccoon dog came out of a wood and said to him: "My dear old man, I am the raccoon dog you kindly saved some time ago. You seem to be in low spirits. Is anything the matter with you?"

"Though the year's end is close at hand, I can hardly buy anything to prepare for the New Year," muttered the old man. "Well then, don't worry," said the raccoon dog. "I shall turn myself into a tea-kettle, so please take it to the village temple though it will be somewhat heavy, and sell it to the chief priest for three 'ryo.' " ('Ryo' — highest unit of the old Japanese coinage.) The old man wondered if such a thing would be possible. But at the insistence of the animal, he finally agreed.

Thereupon, when the raccoon dog rolled its tail and turned a somersault, it changed into a fine bronze tea-kettle in the twinkling of an eye. The old man wrapped it up in cloth and went to the temple.

"Dear abbot, I have obtained a rare article, so I have brought it to you! It is a bronze tea-kettle. Won't you buy it from me?" said the old man. The priest took up the kettle, closely examined it and struck the brim with a finger. It resounded deeply, fascinating the priest. Eager to obtain the tea-kettle, the abbot said to the old man: "What do you ask for it?" "Well, I want three 'ryo,' " replied the old man.

The priest, though considering the price rather high, paid the sum as he thought the excellent kettle was worth the money. Greatly delighted, the old man hurried home to the waiting old woman with three 'ryo.'

Well, you may now wonder what became of the tea-kettle. Now that he had obtained a fine kettle to his liking, the priest wanted to make tea with it and ordered a novice to wash it well. The novice took the kettle to the kitchen, sprinkled sand on it and scrubbed it with a brush. All of a sudden, the kettle said to the young boy: "Ouch, ouch! Dear novice, wash me gently. My bottom aches!"

Dumbfounded, the boy ran to the abbot. "Abbot, sir, the kettle spoke! It told me to wash gently as its bottom ached!"

Unperturbed, the priest replied: "Well, that's because the kettle is so fine it sounds differently. It must have sounded like the human voice. Now stop washing and make hot water with it."

So the novice put water in the kettle, placed the kettle on a kitchen range and lit a fire.

"Too hot, too hot, dear novice! Make a fire slowly," said the kettle again suddenly.

Now greatly scared, the boy scampered to the abbot. "Don't think I am imagining things!" said the novice. "It surely said, 'Too hot, too hot. Make a fire slowly.'"

Still unbelieving, the priest now wanted to drink tea, thinking the hot water was ready. So he directed the boy to stop making a fire and to draw hot water from the kettle.

"Yes, sir," replied the boy and returned to the kitchen. There he saw the kettle suddenly put forth arms, legs and a tail. Startled, the boy fell onto the floor, shouting: "Abbot, sir, a terrible thing has happened!" Thereupon, the priest hurried to the kitchen. Instead of the kettle, he saw a raccoon dog just running out.

This time, he was truly frightened out of his wits, at a loss what to do. And the raccoon dog, crying and stroking its burned bottom, scurried home to its burrow in the mountains.

The Story of a Grateful Crane

(Tsuru no On-gaeshi)

ONCE upon a time, there lived an honest young man in the countryside of Japan.

One day, while he was tilling a paddy field, a crane suddenly came flapping down quietly from the sky. It was a white crane with truly beautiful feathers. Apparently wounded, however, the bird did not fly away, but came reeling toward the man and weakly fell to the ground. Wondering, the man checked the crane's feathers and found an arrow stuck in the base of the wings.

"Poor crane! That's why you can't fly!" So saying, the young man pulled the arrow out and washed the wound clean. The crane soon recovered and showed its delight by flapping its wings. "Now," the man said to the bird, "be careful never to be spotted by a hunter again." Thereupon, the crane circled over his head three times as if to express

62

its thanks and then disappeared high into the sky after uttering a shrill cry. The young man resumed his work, deeply contented that he had done a good thing.

At nightfall when the stars began to appear, he returned to his home. To his great surprise, however, he found a beautiful young woman whom he had never seen before standing at the entrance. She greeted him, saying, "Thank you for your day's hard work." Startled, the man wondered if he was entering the wrong house, but the woman said with a smile, "This is your home and I'm your bride." "I don't believe it," the man shouted. "I'm so poor no woman will ever agree to marry me. Besides, I have only enough rice to feed a single person!" "Don't worry," the woman replied. "I have brought rice." So saying, she took rice out of a small bag and began to fix supper.

The man finally consented, saying, "How strange that you should force me to marry you! Well, do what you like!" And thus the woman came to live with the poor young man. Oddly enough, the small bag the woman had brought always provided the amount of rice they wanted, enabling the couple to lead a happy life.

Time went by and one day, the woman asked her husband to set up a workshop for weaving. He borrowed money and had a special room built. Thereupon, the woman entered the room, saying, "Please never look in here for seven days."

And for exactly seven days after that, only the sound of a loom was heard from within day in and day out. The man felt as if he were waiting for as long as one or two years, but remembering her request, he did not peep into the workshop.

The seven days passed and the woman came out somewhat haggard. Held in her hands was a roll of resplendently beautiful cloth such as he had never hoped to see. "Now," she said to him, "I have woven a roll of cloth. Please take this to the town market. It will sell for 100 'ryo' (a big sum in terms of ancient Japanese coinage)." The next day, the man went to town and the cloth brought a surprisingly high price just as his wife had said. Startled and delighted, he hurried home.

Upon reaching home, he found his wife already closeted in the workshop, and only the sound of the loom was heard. He wondered how she could weave such beautiful cloth apparently without threads. Soon he could no longer contain his ardent desire to see her, and stealthily peeped into the workshop, breaking his promise

65

never to do so.

To his great surprise, he could not find his comely wife there. Only a crane was weaving cloth with white feathers plucked from its body. Promptly realizing that the man was looking in, the crane stopped weaving, staggered toward him and said:

"Well, my dear husband, you have seen everything. Now that you have found out what I really am, I can no longer stay here, to my great regret. I am the crane who

66

was saved by you. To repay your kindness, I have so far served you in the shape of a woman. But from now on, please regard this half-finished cloth as myself and keep it dearly."

The crane then flew up with her remaining wings and vanished into the sky, never to return to the man.

The Japanese Cornucopia

(Shio-fuki Usu)

ONCE upon a time, there lived two brothers in a farming village of old Japan. The elder brother was wishing his younger brother would leave home and marry into a different family. But the latter was a clever man eager to set up an independent home.

Soon the younger brother married, rented a small room and started to eke out a scanty livelihood. As winter came, however, piecework — his source of income — gradually diminished to nil, and on New Year's Eve, the couple had no more rice left. Therefore, he went to his elder brother to borrow one "sho" (1.638 quarts) of rice. But the latter refused, saying scornfully: "How can you keep a wife without a grain of rice?"

Embarrassed, the younger brother walked toward a mountain with a heavy heart. When he reached a moun-

tain pass, he noticed an old man with a white beard collecting firewood.

"Where are you going, young man?" asked the old man. "Well," the younger brother replied, "I'm just strolling aimlessly as I have no rice although we are greeting New Year's Eve tonight." "It's a pity!" the old man said. "I'll give this to you." So saying, he handed a small barley bun to the young man, adding: "Take this to the shrine of the Forest Deity. There is a cave behind the shrine, in which you'll find dwarfs. Anxious to eat the bun, they will implore you to give it to them. So tell them, 'I don't want money. But I'm willing to exchange the bun for the stone mortar.'"

The young man thanked the old man, went to the shrine in the forest and found a cave just as the old man had said. In the cave, a group of dwarfs was making a fuss. Peeping into the cave, he noticed them trying to take in a large river reed, and so, he carried the reed into the depth of the cave for the dwarfs. Delighted, they said: "What a strong man you are!" One of them noticed the barley bun in the hand of the young man and asked him for it, offering a mountain of gold in payment.

But the young man said just as the old man had told

him to: "It's not the money but the stone mortar that I want." The dwarfs then said: "This mortar is a peerless treasure, but it can't be helped. We shall exchange it for the bun," and handed him the stone mortar.

When the young man returned to the pass with the mortar, he found the old man still collecting firewood.

"Well," the old man said, "you have exchanged the bun for the mortar. Now I will teach you how to use it. If you spin the mortar rightward, it will turn out anything you like endlessly with the sole exception of barley buns. And if you want to stop it, just spin it leftward."

Exhilarated, the young man returned home and found his wife in a pout. "Where in the world have you been wandering about despite the approach of New Year's Eve?" she shouted. "Have you obtained anything from your brother?" "Well, well," he said to her, "don't be so peevish. Please spread out a straw mat at once." He put the stone mortar on the mat and turned it rightward, saying: "Rice, come out! Rice, come out!" Thereupon, the mortar poured out rice continuously. Then he said: "Salmon, come out! Salmon, come out!" and the mortar also produced the fish one after another. In this way, he took whatever he needed out of the mortar and the couple spent the happiest New

71

Year's Eve they had ever had.

Upon waking on New Year's Day, he said to his wife: "Now that I am a wealthy man, why should we remain in a rented house?" Then he went about spinning the mortar and obtained a fine house, a big godown, a stable and seven fine horses. Finally, he ordered the mortar to turn out "mochi" (rice cake) and "sake" and invited neighbors and relations to a grand banquet.

All villagers, including his elder brother, were astounded. He was displeased, wondering how his younger brother could become so rich in a single day, and decided to keep a close watch on what he did. Without knowing this, the younger brother quietly entered a neighboring room and spun the mortar, saying: "Candies, come out! Candies, come out!" in order to give candies to the guests by way of a gift. The elder brother saw all this from his hiding place.

After the guests had left and the younger brother and his wife had gone to bed, the elder brother sneaked into the room where the stone mortar lay. He stole not only the mortar but also a large amount of remaining candies and "mochi" and fled. Upon reaching a beach, he found a moored boat. He boarded the vessel and rowed it out to sea for he intended going to a distant place and become wealthy by spinning the mortar. After rowing for quite a while, he became hungry and ate his fill of candies and "mochi." After thus eating sweet things, he wanted to lick some salt. So he spun the mortar rightward, saying: "Salt, come out! Salt, come out!" After taking out some salt, he wanted to halt the spinning mortar but did not know how. The mortar kept on turning, producing salt endlessly. Soon the boat became filled with a mountain of salt, and the weight of the salt finally caused the vessel to sink. And the elder brother also went down with the boat.

There has since been nobody around who can spin the mortar leftward to stop it from turning out salt. So the mortar still continues spinning, on and on, producing salt in a endless flow. That is why the sea is salty, it is said.

The Magic Hood

(Kiki-mimi Zukin)

LONG, long ago in ancient Japan, there lived an old man, poor but honest.

One day while worshiping at the village shrine, he became sleepy because of balmy weather and dozed off to sleep. He had a dream in which a deity with a long white beard appeared and said to him:

"Old man, I will give you something good, as you work hard and are very honest. When you wear this red hood, you can understand the birds' twitterings and the trees' whispers as if they were human beings!" As soon as he finished talking, he disappeared. When the old man was about to say, "Well, thank you very much," he awoke.

To his surprise, the old man found on his lap the same red hood he had seen in the dream; Delighted, he stuffed the hood into the fold of his kimono close to his breast and

75

set out for home. He made such haste he soon tired. So he sat down underneath a pine tree by the roadside.

At that moment, a crow came flying from the east and perched on a branch of the pine tree. Then another crow came flying from the west and also alighted on the branch. And the two birds started croaking to each other.

Pleased that an opportunity of testing the red "Kiki-mimi Zukin" (Listening Hood) had come so soon, the old man took it out and put it on. To his great surprise, he could completely understand all that the birds were saying to each other.

"Mr. West Crow, it's a long time since I saw you last. Is there any news in your village?"

"Well, Mr. East Crow, indeed I haven't seen you for a long time! Nothing particular to speak of . . . Oh, there's one thing. The headman of the western village has been laid up with an illness for some time. But this illness is due to a curse of a snake, which has remained trapped between clapboards of his storehouse since it was built, still painfully trying to get out.

"However, human beings are such foolish creatures, you know, that they still don't understand this! What a pity, don't you think? Well, is there anything new in the

MATSUO
Ikinani

eastern village?"

"Well, I have a similar story. The daughter of the headman of my eastern village is also sick in bed. When the headman had a tea-ceremony room built, a cypress tree on its site was felled down. Since rain water from the eaves falls in drops on the stump of the tree, it is decaying but still alive. Moreover, when the cypress stump puts forth new shoots in the spring, they are instantly snipped off.

77

"So the stump is in great agony, unable either to live or die! And the curse of the cypress tree has made the headman's daughter sick. But how foolish human beings are! They cannot understand this!"

Upon listening to this conversation between the two crows, the old man happily returned home.

The next day, the old man went to the western village. In front of the headman's residence, he called out: "I tell fortunes! I tell anybody's fortune!" Just as he expected, a servant came out and said to him: "Fortune-teller, our master's illness is showing little improvement. Could you see what is wrong?"

The old man entered the headman's room and pretended to meditate for a while, and then said: "You have recently built a storehouse, haven't you? When it was built, a snake was trapped between the clapboards. The snake is still alive but in great agony, so have the creature released from the clapboards. This will certainly cure the master's disease!"

The headman promptly sent for a carpenter. When the clapboards were removed, a lean, almost parched snake was discovered. When the snake was freed, the master's illness healed like magic! Greatly delighted, he gave the old man plenty of money.

And the following day, he went out to the eastern village. Using the same method as on the previous day, he was called into the residence of the village headman to determine the cause of his daughter's illness. That night, he stayed up in the tea-ceremony room. In the dead of night, he heard a rustling sound although there was no wind. He put the red hood on and quietly opened the door.

In the garden, the old man heard a mountain pine tree speaking to the cypress stump. The pine tree was heard to say: "Mr. Cypress, how do you feel today? I think something good will occur this spring, so please stick it out without despairing!"

Next an oak tree spoke words of encouragement to the cypress. After that, all kinds of trees one after another comforted the cypress through the night. The old man wearing the magic hood could understand everything the trees spoke!

The morning arrived, and the old man said to the people of the residence. "Dig up the cypress stump by the tea-ceremony room and transplant it in a spacious area of the garden. If you do so, your daughter's disease will heal instantly." As soon as they did what the old man

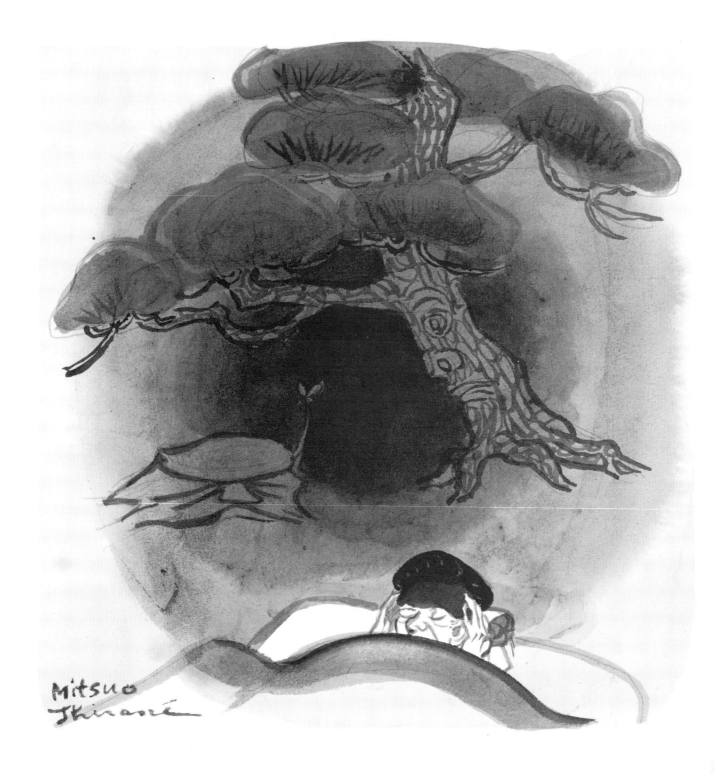

suggested, the daughter got well miraculously. Greatly elated, the headman gave the old man plenty of money and gifts.

Thanks to the "Kiki-mimi Zukin," the old man spent the rest of his life comfortably as a fortune-teller.

The Man Who Married
A Heavenly Maiden

(Hagoromo)

ONCE upon a time, there was a young man in a village who tilled land and collected firewood in the mountains for a living. One day, he went to the mountains to gather firewood together with other villagers. As he finished his work early, he went to a mountain stream to bathe. But he decided to go up the stream farther than where he usually bathed. In the upper reaches of the river where people seldom went, he found a large lake.

There, the young man was surprised to notice a bevy of beautiful maidens bathing in the lake, loudly chatting and laughing. Each girl was a true beauty such as he had never seen before. Delighted, he hid behind a pine tree on the shore. Looking up, he saw beautiful robes, which seemed as light as the feathers of a bird, hanging from a branch. He took one of them and hid himself some dis-

tance away from the lake, waiting for the maidens to finish bathing.

After bathing, the girls put on their robes and disappeared no one knows where. But one of them, unable to find her gown, sat crying at the foot of a pine tree. The young man, who had been watching this from a distance, called out to her: "Is anything the matter?"

The girl, sobbing, said: "I am a 'Heavenly Maiden,'

but while I was bathing, my robe disappeared! So I cannot return to Heaven! . . ." "What a pity!" said the young man. "If you cannot return to Heaven, then please marry me!" Soothing her, he finally cajoled the maiden into accepting his hand and took her home.

Time went by, and a child born between them was now three years old.

One day while lying with the sleeping child, the Heavenly Maiden noticed a timeworn paper parcel hidden behind a crosspiece of the ceiling. Puzzled, she took it down and opening it, she found the robe she had lost while bathing years before. She now realized the robe had been concealed by her husband. A feeling of anger welled up in her, and as she saw the gown in her hands, she became deeply nostalgic, recalling Heaven where she had been born and brought up. Since her husband happened to be away from home, she changed into the heavenly garment and prepared to depart for Heaven with the child under her arm. All of a sudden, a bank of dark clouds descended to take the Heavenly Maiden back to Heaven.

At that very moment, the husband returned home. Astounded, he shouted: "Where are you off to?" The Heavenly Maiden replied: "Though I love you, I must go back to Heaven now that I have regained my gown. If you miss me, please make one thousand 'zori' (straw sandals) and come up to Heaven!" So saying, she boarded the clouds and vanished into the sky.

Left in painful solitude, the husband made "zori" day in and day out, anxious to go up to Heaven as soon as possible. But to make as many as one thousand "zori" was quite an uphill task requiring a long time. And when he completed the 999th "zori," his patience became finally exhausted. At that moment, a bank of dark clouds again descended to take the man aboard. He jumped on board the clouds and started to ascend to Heaven.

Nevertheless, though he came almost within reach of Heaven, he could not go up any farther, for the number of "zori" he had made fell short by one of the specified figure of one thousand. His wife, watching her husband perplexed so near to Heaven, was moved to pity. She put out a wooden pole and drew him up into Heaven.

Although the man thus managed to reach Heaven, the parents of the Heavenly Maiden disliked him and made many difficult demands of him one after another. One day, they ordered the man to draw water with a basket. But the wife furtively spread oilpaper in the basket, enabling the husband to draw water with it. And on another day, the parents ordered him to sow millet seeds in a farm.

But when the man returned home after doing so, they then ordered him to gather the seeds again and bring them home. Though the man was at a loss what to do, the wife released many doves and had them pick up the seeds and bring them back home. With her assistance, he thus managed to tide over the difficulty again.

Finally, however, the man committed an awful error!

In Heaven, it was prohibited to cut and eat melons. For there was the danger that a torrent of water would gush out of the melon, causing a flood.

One hot day, the man, feeling unbearably thirsty, cut a melon despite the ban. When he was about to eat the fruit, however, a spate of water spurted out endlessly, finally flooding Heaven. Being an earthling, he was swept by the flood away from his wife.

And this flood, it is said, has formed the Ama-no-gawa (Heavenly River or the Milky Way as it is called in the Occident) which one sees clearly high up in the night sky in autumn. The man became Altair, while the wife turned into Vega. They are still separated by the Heavenly River, crying for each other.

The Old Man and His Affectionate Son

(Oya-sute Yama)

ONCE upon a time, there lived a son who was very dutiful and devoted to his father. In those days, it is said, there was a law requiring aged parents, who could no longer work, to be carried to and discarded in the mountains.

The affectionate son's father also grew old and was no longer able to work. Now that the time came to discard him, the son one day set out with the father on his back and went deep into the mountains. While being carried on the son's back, the father who loved him dearly, tore off twigs of trees and dropped them to the ground as guiding marks for fear the son might get lost on his way back.

Far up in a mountain, the son spread leaves at a spot which was sheltered from the rain and placed the father on the leaves. "Now, my dear father," he said, "I must bid you

farewell." Thereupon, the father broke off a nearby twig, and showing it to the son, said: "Dear son, lest you should lose your way, I have dropped twigs like this on the ground so that you may find your way. The twigs will guide you home. Now, good-bye, dear son!"

Moved to tears by his father's affection, the son could not leave him behind and carried him back down the mountain.

However, if this became known to the lord of the country, both the parent and the son would be severely punished. So the son dug a cave in the back yard and hid his father there. Every day, he carried meals to his father in the cave, and whenever he obtained a delicacy, he never failed to share it with him.

One day, the lord put up notices in various parts of the country, calling upon the people to submit "ropes made of ashes." Everybody was at a loss how to twist ashes into ropes, and in the village where the dutiful son lived, no one could solve this difficult problem, either.

Upon learning of this, the father said to his son: "Strand a rope tightly and burn it on a board." When the son did just as the father had told him to, a rope of ashes was formed. He took it to the lord and received high praise for having solved the difficult problem.

Shortly after that, the lord showed him a simple wooden pole which retained no traces of its original shape, and ordered him to confirm which end of the pole had been the root. The son brought the pole back home and asked his father what to do. The father said to him: "Put the pole slowly into the water. The end which floats lightly is the head, and the end which tends to dip into the water is the root."

The son tested the pole according to his father's instruction and reported the result to the lord. Impressed with the fine settlement of the second difficult problem as well, the lord warmly praised the son.

However, the lord then came up with a third knotty problem, which was more difficult than the previous two. That is, he ordered the son to make a "drum that can be sounded even without beating."

The son again consulted his father, who immediately replied: "Well, nothing could be easier, son. Go and buy leather. Then go to the mountain and bring a beehive." The son did as instructed and the father made him a drum with the beehive in it. "Take this to the lord," he said to the son.

Promptly, the son took the drum to the lord. When the lord touched the drum, the surprised bees within flew about and bumped into the leather membranes. Consequently, the drum started to sound.

Complimenting the son on the remarkable solution of the three difficult problems in succession, the lord asked him how he could manage to find such wonderful solutions.

MITSUO
Shirane

The son replied: "Being too young to have enough experience and wisdom, I could not work out any of the problems. To tell the truth, I obtained all the solutions from my old father, rich in experience and wisdom." Tearfully, he confided everything, saying: "I could not leave my father behind in the mountain, so I have hidden him in my home."

Impressed with the son's story, the lord said: "Well, I did not know old people were so sagacious and valuable. From now on, nobody will be allowed to cast off old parents in the mountains." After that, it is said, old people spent happy lives together with their young.

Gengoro's Ascent
To Heaven

(Gengoro Buna)

ONCE upon a time, there lived a man by the name of
Gengoro. One day while walking along a river bank,
he picked up a mysterious drum. When he beat the drum,
saying: "Nose, extend! Nose, extend!" his nose
lengthened. And when he said: "Nose, shrink! Nose,
shrink!" and beat the drum, his nose shortened. What a
strange drum! Greatly delighted and amused, Gengoro
took the drum home. He consulted with one of his close
friends, and they decided to set out on a journey with the
drum.

The twosome arrived in a village and saw a pretty
young lady walking on a road. Gengoro whispered: "That
girl's nose, extend!" and beat the drum, using care not to
be seen. Thereupon, the girl's nose lengthened all of a
sudden. Startled and blushing with shame, she covered her

face with hands and ran back home.

She was the only daughter of the wealthiest family in the village. Her parents were deeply worried as their daughter broke down crying with her long nose stretching on the straw-matted floor. Anxious to get her strange disease cured, they called doctors and faith healers, and tried everything they could think of. But the long nose showed no sign of shrinking. As all the family grieved and worried, Gengoro's accomplice, posing as a Shinto priest, showed up at the house and said a prayer for the sake of the daughter, feigning a solemn attitude.

Then he said to the parents: "This is a strange illness which neither Shinto priests nor Buddhist priests nor physicians can cure. I would like to advise you, therefore, to put up notices offering a reward of any amount to whoever would restore your daughter's nose to its original state."

As a proverb goes that "a drowning man will catch at a straw," the parents readily accepted the advice of the man disguised as a Shinto priest and put up notices here and there in the village.

Shortly after that, Gengoro turned up in front of the wealthy family's house, chanting: "Good therapy for

96

nose! Good therapy for nose!" Heartened, the parents promptly called him in.

The daughter's nose was nearly as high as the ceiling. With an air of importance, Gengoro said: "The nose is already so long it can't be cured easily! Anyway, I shall try and heal it." Then he had a folding screen set up around the daughter's bed so that he might not be seen by anybody else. After that, he lightly beat the drum, whispering: "Nose, shrink! Nose, shrink!" Thereupon, the girl's nose started to shorten.

But Gengoro promptly stopped beating the drum and deliberately spent as many as seven days in gradually restoring her nose to the original state. Deeply pleased, her parents gave him a large sum of money by way of a reward. Gengoro and the friend returned home and lived in a happy-go-lucky fashion.

One day he was lying on a field and, to relieve boredom, he thought of checking how far his nose would extend. When he had his friend beat the drum without letup, his nose kept on rising — higher than mountains and then higher than clouds — until finally the tip of his nose could no longer be seen from the ground.

Just at that moment, a carpenter of the heavenly

world happened to be building a bridge across the River of Heaven (the Oriental name of the Milky Way). Suddenly, he noticed a strange thing looking like a wooden stake rising up from the direction of the earth and promptly nailed it to the parapet of the bridge.

Totally unaware of this, Gengoro's friend on the earth continued to beat the drum, chanting: "Nose, shrink!" in order to restore the nose to the original length. However, since the tip of the nose was firmly nailed to the bridge across the River of Heaven, Gengoro was steadily pulled up toward Heaven as his nose shrank. At last, he was raised to the heavenly world. The God of Thunder happened to pass by, unfastened the nose from the parapet and said: "How about working for me?"

Gengoro thus became an assistant for the God of Thunder and ran about on clouds every day, unleashing rain and spreading black clouds.

Whenever Gengoro dumped rain, housewives on the earth took in their washing in hot haste, shouting: "Shower! Shower!" Greatly delighted with the sight of this, he was jovially scampering about on the clouds until finally he missed his step and fell headlong from the heavens right into the center of Lake Biwa in the Omi

region. As soon as he touched the water, he turned into a carp.

Even today, large carp called Gengoro-buna live in Lake Biwa, and people say the fish are the offspring of Gengoro.

Princess From the Moon

(Kaguya Hime)

LONG, long ago, there lived an old man whose job it was to fell and sell bamboo. One day while cutting bamboo, he found one which was giving off light near the root. Wondering, he approached and found a cute baby girl, only about 10 centimeters tall, sitting in the hollow stem of the bamboo where the light came from.

Since the old man and his wife had no children, he immediately brought the baby home and affectionately reared her as their daughter. After that, he often found gold coins in the stems of many of the bamboos he felled. So the old man rapidly became better off.

About three months went by, and the girl grew fast. Not only did she become a full-grown woman but a lady of peerless beauty. She was such a great delight for the old couple that the mere sight of her made them forget all

painful or exasperating experiences. Accordingly, they named their daughter Princess Kaguya (literally, Princess Glittering).

The beauty of Princess Kaguya, which was almost ethereal, rapidly won fame throughout the country. And young, stout men came in swift succession to court her. But she would not see any of them and turned all away. Undaunted and never despairing, however, five suitors

101

came back to seek her hand day in and day out, however often they were turned away. They were all noblemen of very high descent, including an Imperial prince.

The old man wanted to choose a groom from among the five and proposed this to Princess Kaguya. But far from being pleased, she assigned a tough task to each of the five suitors, saying she would marry only the man who could accomplish his job creditably.

The tasks called for the five suitors to present her with a rare gift each — that is, "a stone bowl used by Buddha when he attained enlightenment," "a twig of a tree growing on Mt. Horai on an island at the end of the ocean, which has a silver root and a golden trunk and bears fruit of white jewels," "an absolutely non-inflammable cloth woven with the skin of the 'Fire Rat' said to exist in China," "gems glistening in five colors on the head of 'Ryu' (a dragon)" and "a cowrie born of a swallow."

Out of a fervent desire to win the hand of Princess Kaguya, some of the five noblemen even sacrificed their social position or wealth to discover the specified gifts, and one of them even lost his life. But none of the five suitors succeeded in his quest. This was no wonder, since

all the gifts as desired by Princess Kaguya were nonexistent in this world.

Meanwhile, word of the peerless beauty of Princess Kaguya, who would not marry anybody, finally reached the Emperor's ears. He also wanted to take her for his wife and directed the old man to submit her. This delighted the old man very much, but Princess Kaguya would not consent, even saying she would kill herself if forced to marry the Emperor. But her stern refusal only had the effect of fanning his yearning after her.

One day during a hunting trip, the Emperor dropped in on the old man, took Princess Kaguya by surprise and tried to take her to his palace. Suddenly, however, she disappeared from his sight. Realizing she was not an ordinary woman, the Emperor gave up making an Empress of her and returned to his palace.

Three years passed after that, and Princess Kaguya grew more and more beautiful and attractive. But from around the spring of one year, she came to be seized with a pensive mood on moonlit nights for some unknown reason with her beautiful face showing a shadow of grief. Sometimes, streaks of tears were seen on her cheeks while she watched the moon. As time went by, her grief and sorrow apparently deepened further.

Finally, unable to bear seeing her in such a state any longer, the old man said to Princess Kaguya: "What distresses you so much when you see the moon?" "Well," answered the daughter tearfully, "I have long wanted to tell you this, but have been hesitating so far." And she went on to tell the following story:

"To tell the truth, I have come from the Metropolis of the Moon. I committed a sin, and as a punishment, I have been sent down here to live for a while. Now that I have been absolved of the sin, a mission will come from the Metropolis of the Moon on the moonlit night of August 15 this year to take me back up there (Ed. Note: by the lunar calendar, the moon is full on the night of August 15 when the moon looks most beautiful). So I shall have to bid farewell to you and all others who have been so kind to me all these years. That is why I am so sad tears well up in my eyes."

Astonished to hear such a tale, the old man said: "How can I let you, whom I picked from inside a bamboo and brought up to this day, be snatched away to the world of moon?" Sad and angry, he promptly reported this to the Emperor.

Determined to prevent Princess Kaguya from being

carried away to the world of moon, the Emperor ordered the commanding general of the Imperial Guards to protect the old man's home with 2,000 troops under his command on the night of August 15.

The roofs and garden were virtually filled with troops carrying bows and arrows, ready to shoot down anything that might be found moving even a little in the night sky. And deep inside the house was a specially made secret room where Princess Kaguya was put under close guard.

In the dead of night, the neighborhood of the house suddenly became as bright as in broad daylight. Then from a corner of the sky, a group of persons dressed in strange apparel never before seen in this world came descending on a cloud. The troops tried to shoot arrows but oddly enough, all of them completely lost their fighting spirit.

As the troops just stood aghast and transfixed with none of them moving to shoot, the mission from the moon serenely passed through the garden as if in no man's land, entered the house, took Princess Kaguya out of the secret room and put her on board a flying carriage.

In the vehicle, she shed the dress she had on, and put on a garment brought down by the heavenly mission. In-

stantly, Princess Kaguya crying for grief over parting from

the loved ones changed into an expressionless lady of the world of moon — beautiful but devoid of emotion. And the carriage guarded by the heavenly party slowly ascended toward the moon, leaving behind the 2,000 troops, stationary like dolls, and the weeping old man and woman.

BACKGROUND NOTES

The Peach Boy
(Momotaro)

Momotaro is the representative and most popular folk tale of old Japan.

A peach, which appears in the story, was believed to possess exorcising power in ancient Japan. And this belief apparently formed the basis of this tale.

In the story, demons or "Oni" as the Japanese call them appear as villains. But the Japanese "Oni" is different from the Chinese "Oni," which means the departed spirit of a human being. In Japan, "Oni" signifies a legendary monster which has a terrible figure and inflicts harm and injury upon human beings.

Though possessed of a human shape, the demon has one or two bovine horns on the head and tiger's fangs in the month. The skin color of the monster is either red or blue, and it wears only a small piece of tiger skin. The monster is thus imagined to have a really frightening appearance.

109

The Old Man Who Had His Wen Removed by Goblins
(Kobu-tori Jiisan)

In this story, it is ''tengu'' (imaginary human-shaped goblins who live in the depth of mountains, have long-nosed red faces and wings on their backs and hold feather fans in their hands) that show up and snatch a wen off the face of an old man. There is also a story in which ''Oni'' (demons) appear instead of ''tengu'' to do the same. Grimm's Fairy Tales also include a similar story of wen removal.

The Crab's Revenge
(Sarukani Gassen)

This story is one of Japan's five most renowned folk tales. In the latter part of the story, a plan for avenging the parent crab is deftly worked out, and a similar plot can also be found in some folk tales of Europe and other parts of Asia. It is supposed, therefore, that this story had its origin abroad. However, practical lessons of life — for instance, use of bean paste for curing a burn and the danger of a sewing needle being left in bedclothes — are skillfully woven into the tale to exude a typically Japanese atmosphere.

A Fisherman and the Sea Princess
(Urashima Taro)

The story has three main themes — that is, the story of a turtle repaying the kindness of a man, the story of a fairyland where Urashima was taken, and the story of a treasure with magic power. The first theme is skillfully constructed to give a touch of mystery as it is not revealed until the very last that the turtle is actually the daughter of the Sea God. As for the second theme of a fairyland, the description of the Dragon Palace is so elaborate and minute that the ancient Japanese people's idea of paradise is revealed in full. Regarding the third theme of a strange treasure, the crane, into which Urashima is transformed, and the turtle, which represents the Princess, constitute a combination regarded as a symbol of long life in Japan from ancient times. This combination, it is generally believed, also has an exorcising power. Even today, ornaments of the crane and the turtle are set up sometimes at wedding ceremonies.

The Rabbit and the Raccoon Dog
(Kachi-kachi Yama)

This is a revenge story in which an animal punishes an evildoer on behalf of human beings. But originally, it seems, the first and latter parts of the tale were totally different stories, which were somehow combined into a single story later. That is why the construction of the tale shows a rather weak connection between the first and second halves. At any rate, it is one of the fairy tales most heard and loved by Japanese children from olden times.

The Old Man Who Made Dead Trees Bloom
(Hana-saka Jijii)

This story, it is said, is designed to warn people not to be mere imitators. It consists of three parts, and the last part in which dead trees blossom is vividly symbolic of a sense of a gorgeous, flowery season — the spring in Japan when a large variety of bushes and trees put forth flowers in profusion.

The Old Couple and the Sparrow
(Shita-kiri Suzume)

Old men frequently appear in Japan's ancient folk tales — especially, a combination of a ''good old man'' and a ''bad old man.'' Usually, at the end of a story, the ''good old man'' becomes happy, while the ''bad old man'' is sad. The tale of a sparrow with its tongue snipped off gives a typical example of a warm-hearted ''good old man.'' Moreover, he is contrasted with a greedy ''bad old woman'' instead of a ''bad old man.'' But such a combination is rare. This story is one of Japan's five most celebrated folk tales.

A Midget Who Defeated Goblins
(Issun-boshi)

113

In many of the dwarf stories in Japan's ancient folk tales, a divine spirit appears in the shape of a child and brings happiness to this world. The story of Issun-boshi belongs to this category.

As mentioned in the above story, Issun-boshi stands only 3.3 centimeters tall. There is also a story in which a smaller dwarf only 1.5 centimeters appears. But of all dwarf stories, Issun-boshi is best known among the public. This is probably because it is a very heartening story featuring a dwarf's victory over giant goblins.

The Grateful Raccoon Dog
(Bunbuku Chagama)

This is one of Japan's ancient folk tales about animals requiting favors shown by human beings. But the story of a raccoon dog repaying kindness is rare. In ancient times, people believed raccoon dogs and foxes were given to deluding human beings by assuming various shapes. These animals, therefore, were even hated and feared.

A characteristic of this story is that this raccoon dog appears as a friendly creature repaying a human being's kindness. In particular, the latter half of the story in which the raccoon dog plays an active part is full of a comical touch. Therefore, it still serves as material for various jokes even today. In some places, a fox takes the place of a raccoon dog in similar stories.

114

Incidentally, ''Bunbuku'' in the ''Bunbuku Chagama'' (Bunbuku

Tea-Kettle) is an onomatopoetic word describing the bubbling sound of hot water.

The Story of a Grateful Crane
(Tsuru no On-gaeshi)

Japan has many ancient tales of the same theme — that is, a bird saved by a man repaying the kindness by becoming his wife. Various birds appear in these stories, including the Japanese stork, the wild duck and the pheasant as well as the crane, and many of the tales end in a sorrowful parting of the man and the bird wife. They are considered to have derived from the ancient people's faith in a bird's capability of working miracles.

The Japanese Cornucopia
(Shio-fuki Usu)

115

This tale is often referred to as the "Story of Why Sea Water is Salty." Similar stories are widespread throughout Japan and they have been handed down from generation to generation in various parts of the country with slight variations. It is interesting to note that there are similar tales in Korea, China and Europe. But the origin of these tales and how they spread remain a mystery.

The Magic Hood
(Kiki-mimi Zukin)

Japan has many folk tales of animals which assist human beings in surmounting difficulties or accomplishing their jobs. The "Kiki-mimi Zukin" is one of them. Ancient Japanese people believed that each animal and plant has a spirit of its own and is capable of speaking. A unique feature of the "Kiki-mimi Zukin" is that a magic hood enabling man to comprehend the words of animals and plants is used as a medium of communication between them and human beings.

The Man Who Married a Heavenly Maiden
(Hagoromo)

Japan has many folk tales in which Heavenly Maidens descend to earth to be loved by earthly men and marry them. Ancient people considered the robes of Heavenly Maidens light and soft like the feathers of a bird, calling them ''Hagoromo'' (Robe of Feathers).

So folk tales featuring Heavenly Maidens are called ''Hagoromo-mono'' (stories of Hagoromo). This folk tale is rather complicated because it consists of two sections — ''Hagoromo-mono'' in the first half and the story of two separated stars, Altair and Vega, in the latter half.

The Old Man and His Affectionate Son
(Oya-sute Yama)

This old tale consists of two elements: the story of a son who was faithfully devoted to his father, and an interesting solution of one riddle af-

117

ter another. It is typical of ancient stories which start on a sad note but close with a happy ending.

Moreover, the prime motif of this story is the problem of old people, which is still of great concern in modern society. And it is based on the notion that the aged should be valued because of their rich experience and wisdom. But the story does not strike us as a deliberate preaching of a moral lesson. And this is the best and most attractive point of the tale.

Gengoro's Ascent to Heaven
(Gengoro Buna)

This story is typical of pleasantly humorous tales in Japan. The mysterious drum capable of lengthening or shortening a nose plays an important role in the tale. But in similar stories in certain areas, the spinning wheel plays the same role. That is, when a thread is reeled out, the nose extends, and when a thread is reeled in, the nose shrinks. This is the case with farming areas, especially silk-raising districts.

In some stories, meanwhile, Gengoro after curing the girl's strange disease marries her and leads a happy life. Even in this case, Gengoro ends up in losing his nose. In any case, all folk tales of this type are pleasant and facetious initially but end on a rather pathetic note. This is one of the typical narrative styles in Japan.

The God of Thunder, who appears in the latter part of the story, was considered to be in charge of thunderbolts by the people of ancient Japan. It was imagined that the god, dressed in a loincloth, always carried several small drums attached to his body and beat them when dumping rain.

Princess From the Moon
(Kaguya Hime)

Among Japan's folk tales, this has the richest literary flavor, impressively unifying a world of fantasy in the minds of our forebears and a satire on the society of nobility. This tales was written around the 9th century, becoming the origin of novels in Japan.